D1090727

Aluminum

and the Elements of Group 13

THE PERIODIC TABLE

Nigel Saunders

Heinemann Library
Chicago, Illinois

Design: Ian Winton
Illustrations: Peter Bull and Stefan Chabluk
Picture Research: Vashti Gwynn
Originated by Ambassador Litho, Ltd.
Printed and bound in China by
South China Printing Company

08 07 06 05 04
10 9 8 7 6 5 4 3 2 1

Library of Congress Cataloging-in-Publication Data
Saunders, N. (Nigel)
  Aluminum and the elements of group 13 / Nigel Saunders.
     v. cm. -- (The periodic table)
Includes bibliographical references and index.
Contents: Elements and atomic structure -- The periodic table, aluminum, and the group 13 elements -- Discovering elements with light -- Boron --Aluminum -- Gallium -- Indium -- Thallium -- Find out more.
  ISBN 1-4034-1661-3 (HC), 1-4034-5495-7 (pbk.)
  1. Aluminum--Juvenile literature. 2. Group 13 elements--Juvenile literature. [1. Aluminum. 2. Group 13 elements. 3. Chemical elements.]
I. Title. II. Series.
  QD181.A4S38 2003
  546'.67--dc21
                                    2003010235

Acknowledgments
The author and publishers are grateful to the following for permission to reproduce copyright material:
p. 4 Steve Behr/Corbis; p. 8 Ben Johnson/Science Photo Library; p. 9 George Hall/Corbis; p. 10 Volker Steger/Science Photo Library; p. 11 Tek Image/Science Photo Library; p. 12 David Parker/Science Photo Library; p. 13 David Parker/Science Photo Library; p. 14 top Corbis; p. 14 bottom Sheila Terry/Science Photo Library; p. 16 Duomo/Corbis; p. 17 Tony Craddock/Science Photo Library; p. 19 Vaughan Melzer/Science Photo Library; p. 21 Novosti/Science Photo Library; p. 22 Francis G. Mayer/Corbis; p. 23 Alain Nogues/Corbis; p. 25 Colin Cuthbert/Science Photo Library; p. 27 Adrienne Hart-Davis/Science Photo Library; p. 28 Jeremy Horner/Corbis; p. 29 Charles D. Winters/ Science Photo Library; p. 30 Yann Arthus-Bertrand/ Corbis; p. 31 Carin Krasner/Corbis; p. 33 Charles D. Winters/Science Photo Library; p. 34 Arthur Beck/Corbis; p. 35 James L Amos/Corbis; p. 36 Nigel Rolstone, Cordaiy Photo Library Ltd./Corbis; p. 37 Hulton-Deutsch Collection/Corbis; p. 38 David Parker/Science Photo Library; p. 39 Princess Margaret Rose Orthopaedic Hospital/Science Photo Library; p. 40 Will & Deni McIntyre/Corbis; p. 41 Michael Heron/Corbis; p. 42 Russ Lappa/Science Photo Library; p. 43 Ben Johnson/Science Photo Library; p. 44 David Parker/Science Photo Library; p. 45 George D Lepp/Corbis; p. 46 Lester V. Bergman/Corbis; p. 47 TH Foto-Werbung/Science Photo Library; p. 48 Custom Medical Stock Photo/Science Photo Library; p. 49 David Lees/Corbis; p. 50 Patrick Allen/Corbis; p. 51 Rob Lewine/Corbis; p. 52 Bettmann/Corbis; p. 55 NASA/Corbis; p. 56 CNRI/Science Photo Library; p. 57 CNRI/Science Photo Library

Cover photograph of crushed aluminum cans for recycling, reproduced with permission of Corbis.

The author would like to thank Angela, Kathryn, David and Jean for all their help and support.

Special thanks to Theodore Dolter for his review of this book.

Every effort has been made to contact copyright holders of any material reproduced in this book. Any omissions will be rectified in subsequent printings if notice is given to the publishers.

Disclaimer
All the Internet addresses (URLs) given in this book were valid at the time of going to press. However, due to the dynamic nature of the Internet, some addresses may have changed, or sites may have ceased to exist since publication. While the author and publishers regret any inconvenience this may cause readers, no responsibility for any such changes can be accepted by either author or the publishers.

Contents

Elements and Atomic Structure

All around us are millions of different substances. If you look at your surroundings, you will see plastics, metals, water, and many other solids and liquids. We know there are gases in the air even if we cannot see them, and there are many other gases besides. The list of substances is enormous, but incredibly they all have one thing in common. They are all made from just a few simple components called elements.

Elements and compounds

Elements are substances that cannot be broken down into anything simpler using chemical reactions. About 90 elements occur naturally, and scientists have discovered how to make over 20 more using nuclear reactions. About three-quarters of the elements are metals, such as aluminum, and the rest are nonmetals, such as oxygen. The elements can join together in countless combinations in chemical reactions to make compounds. Aluminum and oxygen, for example, react together to make aluminum oxide, commonly called alumina. Most of the millions of different substances in the world are compounds made up of two or more elements chemically joined together.

▼ *The metal alloy frames, rubber tires, riders' clothing, and even the riders themselves—in fact, everything you can see here—are made from some of the millions of substances in the world.*

Atoms

Every substance, whether it is an element or a compound, is made up of tiny particles called atoms. An element contains just one type of atom, and compounds are made from two or more types of atom joined together. Individual atoms are far too tiny for us to see, even with a microscope. If you could stack eight million aluminum atoms on top of one another, the pile would only be a millimeter high!

Subatomic particles

Atoms are not the smallest things in the universe. They are made from even smaller objects called subatomic particles. The biggest ones, called protons and neutrons, are joined together in the center of the atom, making a nucleus. Electrons are subatomic particles that are even smaller than protons and neutrons. They are arranged around the nucleus in different shells, just as the planets are arranged around the Sun. In fact most of an atom is empty space.

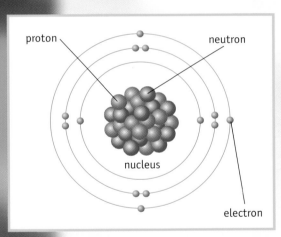

proton
neutron
nucleus
electron

This is a model of an aluminum atom. Each one contains 13 protons and 14 neutrons, with 13 electrons arranged in three shells, or energy levels, around the nucleus.

Groups

Chemistry is both exciting and puzzling because elements all react differently. To help make sense of the reactions, several attempts were made to organize the elements. A Russian chemist named Dimitri Mendeleev was the most successful. In 1869, he placed each element into one of eight groups in a table, making sure that he put similar elements into each group. This made it much easier for chemists to determine how elements might react with one another. The modern periodic table is based closely on Mendeleev's table.

The Periodic Table, Aluminum, and the Elements of Group 13

Chemists have built upon Mendeleev's table, and it has gradually evolved into the periodic table we know today. The elements are arranged in horizontal rows called periods, with the atomic number (number of protons in the nucleus) increasing from left to right. Each vertical column in the periodic table is called a group. The atomic number of the elements increases as you go down a group, and the elements in each group have similar chemical properties. There are eighteen groups altogether.

The number of electrons an element has and the way they are arranged in their shells determine how it reacts. All the elements in a group have the same number of electrons in the shell farthest from the nucleus, which is called the outer shell. The elements in group 1, for instance, are very reactive metals with one electron in their outer shells, whereas the elements in group 17 are reactive nonmetals with seven electrons in their outer shells. The periodic table gets its

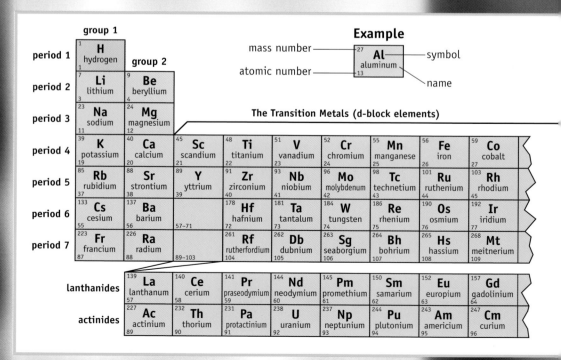

name because these different chemical properties recur regularly, or periodically.

The properties of the elements change gradually as you go down a group. In group 2 the elements become more reactive. When beryllium, which is at the top of the group, is added to water it does not react at all. Calcium, in the middle of the group, slowly produces bubbles of hydrogen, while barium, near the bottom of the group, produces many bubbles.

Aluminum and the group 13 elements

The first element in group 13, boron, is a metalloid, which means that it has some of the properties of metals and some of the properties of nonmetals. The rest of the elements in the group; aluminum, gallium, indium, and thallium, are metals. In this book, you are going to find out about the group 13 elements and many of their uses.

▼ *This is the periodic table of the elements. Group 13 contains boron, aluminum, gallium, indium, and thallium. These elements are all metals, except boron, which is a metalloid.*

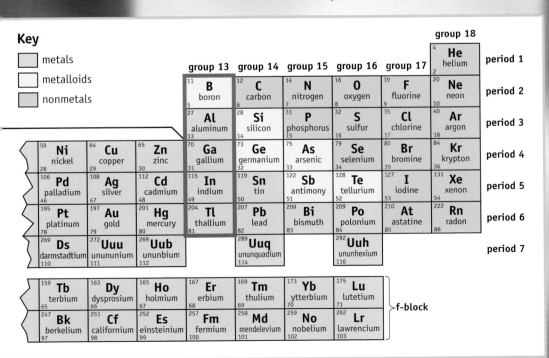

Key

- metals
- metalloids
- nonmetals

			group 13	group 14	group 15	group 16	group 17	group 18
								4 **He** helium 2 — period 1
			11 **B** boron 5	12 **C** carbon 6	14 **N** nitrogen 7	16 **O** oxygen 8	19 **F** fluorine 9	20 **Ne** neon 10 — period 2
			27 **Al** aluminum 13	28 **Si** silicon 14	31 **P** phosphorus 15	32 **S** sulfur 16	35 **Cl** chlorine 17	40 **Ar** argon 18 — period 3
59 **Ni** nickel 28	64 **Cu** copper 29	65 **Zn** zinc 30	70 **Ga** gallium 31	73 **Ge** germanium 32	75 **As** arsenic 33	79 **Se** selenium 34	80 **Br** bromine 35	84 **Kr** krypton 36 — period 4
106 **Pd** palladium 46	108 **Ag** silver 47	112 **Cd** cadmium 48	115 **In** indium 49	119 **Sn** tin 50	122 **Sb** antimony 51	128 **Te** tellurium 52	127 **I** iodine 53	131 **Xe** xenon 54 — period 5
195 **Pt** platinum 78	197 **Au** gold 79	201 **Hg** mercury 80	204 **Tl** thallium 81	207 **Pb** lead 82	209 **Bi** bismuth 83	209 **Po** polonium 84	210 **At** astatine 85	222 **Rn** radon 86 — period 6
269 **Ds** darmstadtium 110	272 **Uuu** unununium 111	269 **Uub** ununbium 112		289 **Uuq** ununquadium 114		292 **Uuh** ununhexium 116		period 7

159 **Tb** terbium 65	163 **Dy** dysprosium 66	165 **Ho** holmium 67	167 **Er** erbium 68	169 **Tm** thulium 69	173 **Yb** ytterbium 70	175 **Lu** lutetium 71	
247 **Bk** berkelium 97	251 **Cf** californium 98	252 **Es** einsteinium 99	257 **Fm** fermium 100	258 **Md** mendelevium 101	259 **No** nobelium 102	262 **Lr** lawrencium 103	f-block

Elements of group 13

The group 13 elements are boron, aluminum, gallium, indium, and thallium. They are all metals except boron. From boron, at the top of the group, to thallium, at the bottom, their boiling points decrease and their densities increase. The group 13 elements are all solids at room temperature, but gallium has a very low melting point compared to the rest. If you hold some gallium in your hand it melts and becomes a liquid.

11 B 5 boron	**boron**
	symbol: B • atomic number: 5 • metalloid

What does it look like? Boron exists in several forms, including hard, gray crystals and a brown powder. Boron does not react with oxygen in the air, unless it is heated strongly, nor does it react with water or hydrochloric acid. However, it will react with concentrated sulfuric acid and nitric acid. Boron is a good conductor at high temperatures, but not at room temperature.

Where is it found? Boron exists naturally as a compound but not as a pure element because it is too reactive. It is found all over the world in various minerals, such as borax, kernite, and colemanite. It was named by joining the first part of the word *borax* with the last part of the word *carbon*.

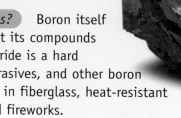

This is a piece of kernite. It contains boron in a compound called sodium tetraborate. Kernite is soft and very light. ▶

What are its main uses? Boron itself has very few uses, but its compounds have many. Boron nitride is a hard substance used in abrasives, and other boron compounds are found in fiberglass, heat-resistant glass, detergents, and fireworks.

27		aluminum
Al		symbol: Al • atomic number: 13 • metal
aluminum		
13		

What does it look like? Aluminum is a strong, silvery metal. It is very malleable, which means that it is easy to shape. It has a low density, so pieces of aluminum feel light for their size. Although aluminum is a very reactive metal, when covered by a layer of aluminum oxide it stops reacting with air or water. However, it will react with hydrochloric acid and sulfuric acid, especially if it is heated.

Where is it found? Aluminum is the most abundant metal in the Earth's crust, but is too reactive to be found as a pure metal. It is present in many minerals, including bauxite and cryolite. Bauxite, which contains aluminum oxide, is its main ore.

What are its main uses? Aluminum and its alloys have many uses, such as in aircraft, bicycles, and window frames, in containers to store drinks and food, and inaluminum cables, which conduct electricity over long distances. Precious stones, such as rubies and sapphires, are made from aluminum compounds. Other compounds are used in water treatment plants, antiperspirants, and medicines to treat upset stomach.

▼ *Strong aluminum alloys are used to make aircraft such as this Boeing 730-330. These alloys are strong and have a low density, so they help to reduce the weight of the aircraft.*

N949WP

More Elements of Group 13

70	
Ga	
gallium	
31	

gallium
symbol: Ga • atomic number: 31 • metal

What does it look like?   Gallium is a soft, silvery metal. It is solid at room temperature but becomes a liquid above 29.7 °C (85.8 °F). Gallium reacts slowly with damp air at first, forming a layer of gallium oxide on its surface. This layer prevents gallium from reacting with water, but it still reacts slowly with hydrochloric acid.

Where is it found?   Gallium compounds occur widely in Earth's crust. They are found in small amounts in many minerals, including bauxite (aluminum ore).

What are its main uses?   Many gallium compounds, especially gallium arsenide, are important semiconductor materials. Semiconductors are used in a huge range of everyday electronic products, including CD players and solar cells that power calculators.

▲
Light-emitting diodes (LEDs) contain gallium nitride. LEDs give off light when electricity is passed through them.

115	
In	
indium	
49	

indium
symbol: In • atomic number: 49 • metal

What does it look like?   Indium is another silvery metal that is very soft. It does not react with air (unless it is heated strongly) or with water, but it does react with acids.

Where is it found? Indium does not exist as a free metal in the Earth's crust. There are no indium minerals, but small amounts of indium compounds are present in many minerals, especially zinc ores.

What are its main uses? Indium alloys are used in lead-free solders that join electronic components together. Indium compounds are used in the liquid crystal displays, found in many everyday items such as digital watches and electronic games.

The liquid crystal displays (LCDs) used in electronic devices, such as cell phones, CD players, and digital watches, have a layer of transparent indium-tin oxide, which conducts electricity.

204	
Tl	**thallium**
thallium	*symbol: Tl • atomic number: 81 • metal*
81	

What does it look like? Thallium is a bluish, silvery metal that is soft enough to cut with a knife. It reacts slowly with oxygen in the air to form a thick layer of blue-gray thallium oxide. Thallium reacts slowly with water and acids.

Where is it found? Thallium is found in a few rare minerals, such as lorandite (thallium arsenic sulfide), and is usually extracted as a byproduct of zinc production.

What are its main uses? Thallium metal has no commercial uses, but its compounds are used in radiation detectors and in special glass that has a very low melting point.

Discovering Elements with Light

Two German chemists, Gustav Kirchhoff and Robert Bunsen, discovered cesium in 1860 by analyzing the light it emits. Three metals in group 13, gallium, indium, and thallium, were discovered within fourteen years of each other using this method, which is known as spectroscopy.

This is Gustav Kirchhoff (1824–1887). Working with Robert Bunsen, he discovered cesium and rubidium by studying the spectra of light given off by compounds when they are heated strongly. ▶

Flame tests

Kirchhoff was the first person to realize that metals produce different colors when their compounds are burned in a flame. Flame tests allow chemists to determine which metal is in an unknown compound. In a flame test, some of the compound is put on a loop of clean platinum wire and held in the hottest part of the Bunsen burner flame. The color of the resulting flame depends on the metal in the compound.

Excited electrons

When an atom is heated, its electrons use the extra energy to jump into a shell farther from the nucleus. Electrons cannot stay in this excited state for long and soon fall back to a shell closer to the nucleus. They give off their extra energy as light; long falls give out blue light and short falls give out red light. Each element produces different colors because its electrons can make different jumps and falls.

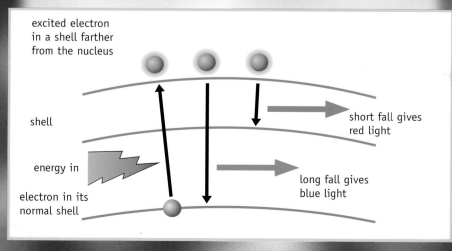

excited electron in a shell farther from the nucleus

shell

short fall gives red light

energy in

long fall gives blue light

electron in its normal shell

Spectroscopy

In spectroscopy, the light given off in a flame test is analyzed using a device called a spectrometer. The simplest spectrometer contains a prism to split light from the flame into its spectrum. Each element produces a unique spectrum of colors, similar to a colored bar code. Kirchhoff and Bunsen discovered cesium when they found some compounds that produced a spectrum they had not seen before. They named the new metal after the Latin for word for "sky blue," because its spectrum contains two blue lines.

Prisms and light

Sir Isaac Newton investigated light in the 1600s. He discovered that white light is made from the colors of the rainbow. Newton found that a prism splits light up into a spectrum, displaying the different colors it contains.

◀ White light is a mixture of all the different colors we see. When a beam of white light is shined through a glass prism, the light is split up to make a spectrum.

Gallium, indium, and thallium

Sir William Crookes discovered thallium in 1861. He named the new metal after the Greek word meaning "green twig" because its spectrum contains a clear green line. Indium was discovered two years later by the German chemists Ferdinand Reich and Theodor Richter. Indium is named after the Latin word for "indigo" because its spectrum contained an indigo (very dark blue) line.

Paul-Emile Lecoq, a French chemist, discovered gallium in 1875. Although gallium's spectrum contains violet lines, Lecoq named the element after the Latin name for France, which is *Gallia*.

Boron

Boron is a metalloid, which means that it has some properties of metals and some of nonmetals. For instance, it is a poor conductor of electricity at room temperature, but a good conductor at high temperatures and it can react with both metals and nonmetals. Boron reacts with concentrated sulfuric acid and nitric acid, but not with hydrochloric acid or water. It only reacts with oxygen in the air if it is heated strongly. There are several forms of boron, including a dull brown powder and shiny gray crystals.

Crystalline boron is shiny and gray. Compounds containing boron are found in heat-resistant glass, detergents, and the control rods for nuclear power plants. ▶

Discovery of boron

Boron was discovered in 1808, but boron compounds such as borax have been used for hundreds of years. Boron was discovered twice. Sir Humphry Davy, an English chemist, heated potassium with boric acid and produced brown powdered boron. At about the same time, two French chemists, Joseph-Louis Gay-Lussac and Louis-Jacques Thénard, carried out similar experiments. Davy called the new element boracium and the French called it bore.

This is the French chemist Joseph-Louis Gay-Lussac (1778–1850), who was one of the first chemists to isolate boron. ▶

14

After studying the new element's chemical reactions, Davy decided that it was not a metal after all, so its name should not end in *ium* (this word ending usually refers to metals, except for helium, which is a nonmetal). Four years later Davy suggested the name boron because it is similar to carbon.

Davy's experiments with electricity

An Italian scientist named Alessandro Volta invented the electric battery at the end of the 1700s. Humphry Davy was one of the first chemists to find out what happens when electricity is passed through different substances. After building his own battery, Davy used it to discover sodium and potassium in 1807 and to isolate magnesium, calcium, strontium, and barium a year later. Davy also isolated some boron in 1808 by passing electricity through boric acid.

Extracting boron

On average every ton of rock contains 9 grams (0.32 ounces) of boron. It is found in various minerals, such as borax, colemanite, and kernite. Some natural spring water contains boric acid. Boron minerals have many uses. The relatively little boron that is extracted requires several steps, including heating boron oxide with magnesium to produce impure powdery boron.

> *The equation for producing boron from boron oxide is*
>
> boron oxide + magnesium → boron + magnesium oxide
>
> $$B_2O_3(s) + 3Mg \rightarrow 2B(s) + 3MgO(s)$$

If very pure crystals of boron are needed, boron chloride is heated with hydrogen using very hot wires.

> *The equation for producing boron from boron chloride is:*
>
> boron chloride + hydrogen → boron + hydrogen chloride
>
> $$2BCl_3(g) + 3H_2(g) \rightarrow 2B(s) + 6HCl(g)$$

Uses of boron

Powdered boron burns with a green flame and is used in fireworks and green signal flares. However, boron has many other uses, including the production of advanced composite materials and alloys.

Boron fibers

Very fine boron fibers can be used to produce extremely tough, lightweight materials. They are made by heating very fine tungsten wires in a mixture of boron chloride and hydrogen at over 1000 °C (1832 °F). Boron chloride and hydrogen react to produce tiny crystals of pure boron, which form on the tungsten wires. The boron fibers are usually about as thick as a human hair. They cannot be used on their own, but must be set in another substance, such as metal or plastic.

Composite materials

Composite materials are made by combining two very different materials to produce a new substance. Usually this substance has better properties than either material on its own. Resin, for example, may be too weak to make a tennis racquet, but when combined with boron fibers it forms a strong, lightweight material.

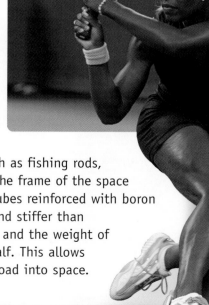

Boron fibers set in various plastic resins are used in aircraft, the hulls of racing boats, and sports equipment, such as fishing rods, golf clubs, and tennis racquets. The frame of the space shuttle is made from aluminum tubes reinforced with boron fibers. This material is stronger and stiffer than aluminum, so less of it is needed and the weight of the tubes is reduced by almost half. This allows the shuttle to carry a bigger payload into space.

Boron in alloys

Most of the metals we see around us are not pure metals, but alloys. Alloys are mixtures of different metals or metals mixed with nonmetals or compounds. The alloys produced by adding boron or boron compounds to metals are usually harder than the metal alone. Steel mixed with boron and titanium produces a very tough alloy that is often used for security chains, such as the expensive chains that go with bicycle locks. Large earth-moving vehicles and excavators need tough metal blades to scrape away soil. The steel used in these blades contains tiny amounts of boron to increase its strength and toughness.

◀ *Boron steel is tougher and stronger than ordinary steel, so it is used in the blades of excavators and other earth-moving equipment.*

Aluminum is widely used to make high-voltage electricity cables. However, its ability to conduct electricity is reduced if it contains even small amounts of other metals, such as iron and titanium. If boron is added in the right amounts to react with these impurities, a slag is produced that is easily separated from the aluminum.

◀ *Tennis racquets (opposite) and other sports equipment such as golf clubs and fishing rods may be strengthened with boron fibers set in special plastic resins.*

Boron and Nuclear Reactions

Boron is very good at absorbing neutrons produced by nuclear reactions, which makes it especially useful for controlling the reactions in nuclear reactors.

Neutrons will break us apart

Chemical reactions involve the electrons around the nucleus, but nuclear reactions involve the nucleus itself. Nuclear fission is the type of nuclear reaction used in nuclear reactors. This is when atoms in the reactor's nuclear fuel split apart. Uranium is used as a nuclear fuel because its atoms can be split apart relatively easily.

When a uranium atom splits it produces two smaller atoms, some heat and radiation, and two or three neutrons. These neutrons shoot out at high speed and smash into other uranium atoms. These atoms may split too, producing even more neutrons. This is called a chain reaction and must be controlled. If it is not, so much energy is released in a short time that a nuclear explosion happens.

Controlling the reaction

A nuclear reaction will carry on at a steady pace if each uranium atom that splits causes one more to split. When this occurs, the reaction is said to be critical. In a nuclear reactor, the reaction needs to remain at the critical level. Reactions are controlled by means of control rods made from boron steel or boron carbide. Boron absorbs neutrons, which prevents them from splitting uranium atoms. Boron control rods that are lowered directly into the reactor absorb so many neutrons that the chain reaction stops. However, the rods are usually lifted out of the reactor until the reaction continues at the correct rate.

The first nuclear reactor

The first nuclear reactor was built at the University of Chicago and started up on December 2, 1942. An Italian-born American physicist named Enrico Fermi led the team that built it. Element number 100 is called fermium in his honor.

Boron effectively slows down nuclear reactions by absorbing
neutrons. Above are some of the 211 boron carbide control rods
used in the nuclear power plant near Chernobyl, in the Ukraine.
When too few of these were left in the reactor in April 1986,
disaster ensued.

Nuclear reactors and electricity

The heat produced by the nuclear reaction is used to boil
water to make steam. This drives turbines, just as in a
conventional power plant that burns coal, gas, or oil. The
turbines turn electricity generators and provide factories and
millions of homes with electricity. Over several months, the
nuclear fuel is slowly used up and the reaction slows down.
The boron control rods are gradually lifted higher to keep
the reaction going until some of the spent fuel must be
replaced. If anything goes wrong with the reactor, the boron
control rods drop down automatically, stopping the reaction
within seconds.

Life-Saving Boron

The nuclear reaction in a reactor is controlled by lowering or raising control rods that contain boron. If the control rods are lifted out, the reaction goes faster and if they are lowered, it slows down. However, what would happen if nearly all the control rods were lifted out at once?

The Chernobyl disaster

The Chernobyl nuclear power plant was 15 kilometers (9 miles) from Chernobyl, a town 100 kilometers (62 miles) north of Kiev, in the Ukraine. Mistakes made by the operators during an experiment added to a design fault in the reactor and caused the nuclear reaction to destabilize.

The reactor used 211 boron carbide control rods. At least 30 had to be in the reactor for it to be safe. At one point, early in the morning of April 26, 1986, the operators left only 8 control rods in the reactor, and the nuclear reaction went out of control. All the control rods were dropped back into the reactor, but this pushed cooling water out of the way, making things worse. An enormous amount of heat was produced, which melted the uranium fuel and turned the water to steam. The pressure from the steam caused an explosion that wrecked the reactor and blew off its 1,000-ton lid. Graphite in the core of the reactor ignited and released huge amounts of radioactive chemicals that were carried by winds and air currents throughout Europe and beyond.

Boron to the rescue

It took several days to put out the fires at the Chernobyl reactor. Helicopters dumped a mixture of boron carbide, lead, sand, and other materials over the fire. The boron carbide captured neutrons to stop any further nuclear reactions, and the lead absorbed the radiation. Nearly 1,000 people were involved in firefighting, and 800,000 soldiers helped clean up after the accident. Many of these people and the local population were exposed to large amounts of radiation. Radiation damages cells and the DNA in them, causing illnesses such as cancer. Some people died and many still suffer from illnesses linked to the radiation.

▲

These are the remains of the Chernobyl nuclear power plant after it exploded in the early hours of April 26, 1986.

Killing cancer cells

Boron neutron capture therapy (BNCT) is a treatment for cancer. Doctors inject the patient with a boron compound that concentrates in cancer cells. A machine called a particle accelerator is used to fire neutrons at the cancer. When a boron atom in a cancer cell absorbs a neutron, it splits in two and gives off alpha radiation. This type of radiation does not travel far, so the cancer cells are killed, but not the healthy cells around them.

Borates

Boron forms several different compounds with oxygen, including borax and boric acid. These different compounds can be converted into each other and in industry the word *borates* is used loosely for all of them.

Borax

Borax is the common name for sodium tetraborate decahydrate ($Na_2B_4O_7 \bullet 10H_2O$). A colorless solid with a soft, slippery feel, it is the most important source of boron compounds. Nearly half the world's borax comes from California. Boric acid (H_3BO_3) is made by reacting concentrated borax solution with hydrochloric acid. Boric oxide (B_2O_3) is formed when boric acid is heated. These compounds and others, such as sodium perborate ($NaBO_3$), have a great many uses.

Tincal

In the Middle Ages, borax was extracted from salt lakes in Tibet. Called tincal, it was used to make pottery glazes.

Glazes

Pottery and tiles are covered with a hard, glassy substance called a glaze. Glazes are usually colored, smooth, and shiny, giving the object a tough, attractive finish that is difficult to scratch. Borates are added to help the pigments dissolve in the glaze, to stick the glaze to the pottery, and to make it more resistant to water and cleaning chemicals.

The glazes used on tiles and pottery, like this vase, contain boron compounds. They produce a smooth, tough finish that resists water and cleaning fluids.

Steel and other metals can be coated with a tough type of glaze called enamel that also contains borates. Enameled steel sheet is used to make the sides of washing machines and dishwashers. Other items found in the kitchen, such as pans and coffeepots, may be enameled. Hikers and campers often use enameled cups and plates.

Helping keep clean

Borates are widely used in household detergents and soaps, including those for washing machines and dishwashers. They soften the water, which improves the cleaning power of the detergent and prevents sticky scum from forming. Sodium perborate may be added as a bleach to remove stains from clothes and dishes. Shampoos, bath salts, and liquid soaps contain borates, which improve their consistency and remove oils and other dirt from the skin and hair.

Glass and glass fibers

Borosilicate glass is very tough and heat resistant. It is made by adding boric acid to sand, which is the main ingredient for making glass. This type of glass is used to make beakers and test tubes for chemistry laboratories and kitchen glassware, such as pitchers, bowls, and ovenware. The main use for borates is in the manufacture of glass fiber. This consists of very fine strands of glass made by squeezing molten glass through small holes. Glass fiber is used as heat insulation in homes. Woven glass fibers are mixed with plastic resins to make fiberglass objects such as canoes and surfboards.

◀ Boron compounds are widely used in the manufacture of glass fiber. This substance is used to insulate buildings and to make tough fiberglass objects such as bathtubs and boats.

Borates and Black Diamonds

Boron can form complex compounds, called boranes, with itself and hydrogen. Diborane (B_2H_6) is a poisonous and explosive gas, which is used by computer chip manufacturers to provide the tiny amounts of boron required by some silicon chips.

Boron carbide is used in the control rods for nuclear power stations because it is good at absorbing neutrons, but it has other important properties.

Black diamond

Boron carbide is made by heating boron oxide with carbon in a furnace. It is sometimes called black diamond because it is very hard, like real diamond, and is a good abrasive. Manufacturers of computer hard disk drives use boron carbide for polishing disks. Nozzles for sandblasting hoses, bullet-proof seats for helicopters, and armored tiles for military vehicles are also made from boron carbide. Boron carbide body armor is much lighter than similar armor made from other materials, such as steel. Boron carbide is also mixed with metals to produce very hard alloys that are used to make tough cutting blades.

The equation for the manufacture of boron carbide is

boron oxide + carbon ⟶ boron carbide + carbon monoxide

$$2B_2O_3(s) + 7C(s) \longrightarrow B_4C(s) + 6CO(g)$$

Boric acid (H_3BO_3) may be used instead of boron oxide.

White graphite

Boron chloride heated with ammonia (NH_3) makes boron nitride. Like boron carbide, boron nitride resists attack from other chemicals and has a high melting point. It has a slippery feel and makes a good lubricant, so it is sometimes called white graphite. Real graphite is a form of pure carbon used in pencils because layers of graphite slide onto paper, leaving a mark. Powdered boron nitride is used to produce a silky feel in face powders and lipsticks. Boron nitride is a good conductor of heat, and it is an important component of thermal pastes used for computer chips.

Modern computer chips generate a lot of heat as they work. If this heat is not removed from the chip, the computer may not function properly, and some very fast chips may even catch fire! To prevent this, a heat sink is attached to the surface of the chip. A typical heat sink has spikes or vanes to conduct heat away and is often made from aluminum because it is lightweight and a good heat conductor. Thermal paste, containing boron nitride powder, is smeared over the surface of the chip before the heat sink is attached to it, ensuring that heat is conducted from the chip to the heat sink efficiently.

▲
The processor chips in modern computers produce large amounts of heat. Heat is carried away from the chips using aluminum heat sinks and fans. Special paste that contains boron nitride helps to conduct heat from the chips to the heat sinks efficiently.

Boron in Living Things

Plants and animals need boron to stay healthy, but only in small amounts because some boron compounds are poisonous, especially those that dissolve in water.

Fertilizers and herbicides

Plants need boron to help them transport sugars and make cell walls. When there is not enough boron in the soil, the fruits, stems, leaves, or roots of a plant may crack on the surface and rot in the center. The heads of cauliflowers turn dark, for example. Farmers use artificial fertilizers containing boron compounds on soil that does not contain enough boron. Roots can only absorb minerals that are dissolved in water, and so fertilizers usually contain soluble boron compounds, such as sodium borate and borax. However, farmers need to add just the right amount of these fertilizers because too much boron will poison the plants, turning the leaves yellow. Some valuable crops, such as grapes and strawberries, are particularly sensitive to excess boron. In fact, boric acid and other boron compounds are used in herbicides, which are chemicals that kill weeds.

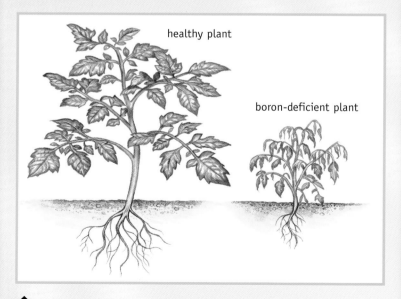

healthy plant

boron-deficient plant

▲
If there is not enough boron in the soil, the walls around plant cells do not form properly and the plants do not grow very well.

Boron in our diet

Too much boron is poisonous, but tiny amounts of it are needed in our diet. Many foods are rich in boron, including raisins, peanuts, popcorn, and chocolate, so we are unlikely to suffer from boron deficiency. Unlike many other trace minerals, no particular symptoms of boron deficiency are known and there is no recommended daily dose. However, there is some evidence that boron may protect us from arthritis, a disease that causes inflammation, pain, and stiffness in the joints. On average fewer people seem to suffer from arthritis in areas where their diet is naturally rich in boron, while more people seem to suffer from it when their diet contains very little boron. However, there is no medical evidence overall that suggests we should deliberately take extra boron in our diet to stay healthy.

Some foods, such as chocolate, raisins, and peanuts are rich sources of boron.

Sick of boron

Excessive exposure to boron can cause diarrhea and peeling, red skin. Large amounts of it cause low blood pressure, vomiting, and hair loss. Although this is unlikely to happen in our everyday lives, people who handle boron compounds in their jobs wear masks and gloves and follow regulations that ensure that boron compounds are disposed of properly.

Pests and pesticides

Boric acid is used in some pesticides, or chemicals that kill undesirable insects such as cockroaches, ants, and termites. When the insects walk through the pesticide powder, it sticks to their legs and is swallowed when they clean themselves.

Aluminum

Aluminum is a strong, silvery metal that is malleable and has a low density. Its surface is covered with a very thin, transparent layer of aluminum oxide that stops the aluminum from reacting with air or water. However, aluminum will react with hydrochloric acid, especially if it is heated. Powdered aluminum will burn with orange sparks if it is sprinkled into a Bunsen burner flame.

This is the famous Statue of Eros at Piccadilly Circus in London. It was cast from aluminum in 1893, when aluminum was still regarded as a rare, expensive new metal. ▶

Saved by the oxide

A very thin, transparent layer of aluminum oxide forms naturally on the surface of aluminum and sticks tightly to the metal. This blocks oxygen and water from reaching the metal beneath, so aluminum seems to be less reactive than it really is. When pieces of aluminum are dropped into warm hydrochloric acid, nothing seems to happen at first. However, the acid reacts with the layer and removes it. Once the metal is exposed, it reacts vigorously with the acid, producing aluminum chloride and many hydrogen gas bubbles.

Discovery of aluminum

Aluminum compounds have been used for thousands of years. Potassium aluminum sulfate forms crystals called alum, which was widely used to help dyes stick to cloth. Chemists were confident that alum and other compounds really did contain a new metal. Aluminum was finally discovered in 1825 by the Danish chemist Hans Christian Oersted, when he heated some aluminum chloride with potassium dissolved in mercury.

The equation for the extraction of aluminum using potassium is

aluminum chloride + potassium → aluminum + potassium chloride

$$AlCl_3(s) + 3K \rightarrow Al(s) + 3KCl(s)$$

The reaction happens because potassium is more reactive than aluminum and displaces aluminum from its compounds.

You say aluminum ...

The new metal was first named alumium after the Latin word for the crystals we call alum. Its name later changed to aluminum, and then became aluminium. In 1925, the American Chemical Society decided to stick with the spelling *aluminum*. The rest of the English-speaking world spells it *aluminium*.

Abundant aluminum

Aluminium is the most abundant metal and forms 8.2 per cent of the Earth's crust. It is found in various **minerals,** such as bauxite and cryolite. Aluminium is difficult to **extract** from its compounds because it is a reactive metal.

◀ *The Danish scientist Hans Christian Oersted (1777–1851) shown here with an assistant, works on an experiment involving electricity and magnetism. Oersted discovered aluminum in 1825.*

Aluminum Extraction and Recycling

Bauxite is aluminum's main ore and contains aluminum oxide. It is mined in huge quantities, mainly in South America, the Caribbean, Australia, and Africa. Over 24 million tons of aluminum are produced each year worldwide.

Alumina

Bauxite contains other substances as well as aluminum oxide, which have to be removed. In the Bayer process, the bauxite is treated with sodium hydroxide solution. This produces a white powder called alumina, which is purified aluminum oxide. The waste material mostly contains iron oxide and sand. It is called red mud because of its color.

This huge bauxite mine is in Venezuela. Much of the land disturbed by the world's bauxite mines was originally covered by forests. With care and a lot or work, new trees can be planted after a mine closes.

Pass the electricity

Aluminum is extracted using electrolysis. This involves passing electricity through molten alumina, causing it to break down into aluminum and oxygen. Unfortunately, alumina has a very high melting point (over 2000 °C, or 2632 °F). A lot of energy would be needed to reach this temperature, so the alumina is dissolved in a mineral called cryolite, which melts at a much lower temperature.

Cryolite

Cryolite (Na_3AlF_6) is a mineral that melts at just over 1000 °C (1832 °F). Alumina dissolves in molten cryolite and as a result does not have to be melted. This method reduces the temperature needed to extract aluminum to around 950 °C (1742 °F), saving energy and money.

The molten mixture of alumina and cryolite is contained in a large pot lined with graphite. Graphite, a type of carbon that conducts electricity well, forms the negative electrode. Graphite blocks lowered into the pot form the positive electrodes. An electric current is passed through the molten mixture between the lining and the blocks. This causes molten aluminum to form at the lining while oxygen gas bubbles off at the positive electrode. The metal sinks to the bottom of the pot from where it is removed, cooled, and solidified.

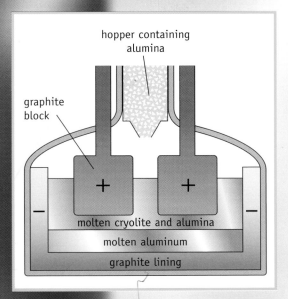

hopper containing alumina

graphite block

+   +

−   −

molten cryolite and alumina

molten aluminum

graphite lining

◀ *This diagram shows how aluminum is extracted by electrolysis.*

Expensive aluminum

Even though there is a lot of aluminum in the Earth's crust, extracting it is fairly expensive. This is because sixteen kilowatt-hours of electricity—enough energy to run a 100-watt light bulb for nearly a week—is needed to produce a kilogram of aluminum. This is why aluminum smelters are often built in areas where electricity is cheap and plentiful.

Although aluminum is extracted at 950 °C (1742 °F), its melting point is 660 °C (1220 °F). This means that far less energy is needed to melt and recycle aluminum. Over a third of the aluminum needed is from recycled sources.

◀ *Aluminum is used to make drink cans like these, which are collected for recycling. A lot of energy is needed to produce aluminum from its ore, so over a third of the aluminum we use comes from recycled metal.*

Uses of Aluminum

In the mid-1800s aluminum was more valuable than gold. Visitors to the 1855 Paris Exhibition marveled at an exhibit of aluminum, and Napoleon III had a special set of cutlery made from the new metal, reserved only for very important visitors. Fortunately, its value fell dramatically after the Hall-Héroult process to extract aluminum was developed in 1886.

The Hall-Héroult process

The modern process for extracting aluminum from alumina was invented by two men working on opposite sides of the Atlantic. Charles Hall in the United States and Paul Héroult in France came up with the idea at the same time in 1886.

Super-pure aluminum

If aluminum is more than 99.9 percent pure, it is called super-pure aluminum. This is a very shiny material used to make the reflective coatings on light fittings, like those used for modern, low-voltage halogen lighting. Metallic inks and paints, including those used for car bodywork, contain powdered super-pure aluminum. Different effects are achieved by varying the size and shape of the aluminum grains in the paint. Metal objects such as car wheels can be coated with aluminum to give a shiny finish, similar to chromium plating.

Into space with aluminum

The space ahuttle and the *Ariane* 5 rocket both use solid rocket boosters. Each space shuttle booster contains about 80 tons of aluminum powder, and the smaller *Ariane* 5 boosters have forty tons. Powdered aluminum will burn if heated to over 1000 °C (1832 °F) in a flame. The oxygen needed for the aluminum to burn is supplied by ammonium perchlorate powder (NH_4ClO_4). The ammonium perchlorate is mixed with the aluminum powder and a chemical called butadiene is added to stick it all together.

Weld those rails

When aluminum powder is mixed with iron oxide powder and heated, they react to produce aluminum oxide and iron. The reaction is very vigorous with a lot of flames, smoke, and heat. So much heat is produced that the iron melts. This is called the thermit reaction and is useful for joining railway track rails together.

Aluminum is also used in reactions like this to extract chromium and vanadium from their ores.

◀ There is a very dramatic reaction between powdered aluminum and iron oxide when they are heated together. So much heat is produced that the iron formed during the reaction melts.

The equation for the thermit reaction is

aluminum + iron oxide → aluminum oxide + iron

$$2Al(s) + Fe_2O_3(s) \rightarrow Al_2O_3(s) + 2Fe(l)$$

Aluminum is more reactive than iron, so it is able to displace iron from iron compounds.

Aluminum in the Home

Aluminum is usually mixed with other metals to produce alloys that are harder and stronger than aluminum alone. Aluminum alloys can be seen in action all around us, especially in our homes.

Hold your drink

Drink cans are made from aluminum containing a small amount of manganese, which increases its strength and makes it easier to press into shape. Pure aluminum is not poisonous and does not rust, but drink cans are usually lined with a very thin layer of plastic. This ensures that the acids and salts in beverages never come into contact with the aluminum. Aluminum has a low density, so the cans are lighter than glass bottles or steel cans. This makes them easier to carry, saves energy when they are transported, and helps when they are collected for recycling.

Eat up

Aluminum foil is very thin aluminum alloy sheet, widely used for storing and cooking food. The metal is passed through rollers until it reaches the desired thickness. Foil for a food container is around 0.07 millimeter (0.003 inch) thick, while aluminum foil is even thinner than this.

Aluminum foil conducts heat well and prevents moisture from escaping when food is baked in the oven. It can be wrapped around sandwiches and other foods, helping to keep them fresh. Many frozen or chilled prepared foods are supplied in aluminum foil containers.

Aluminum foil conducts heat well and prevents moisture from escaping, so it is very useful for storing or cooking food. ▶

Pouches for dried foods, such as dehydrated soup, and cartons for liquids, such as orange juice, are made from plastic or cardboard lined with aluminum foil. Many saucepans are made from aluminum. They are light, strong, and rustproof.

A good reflector

Shiny aluminum foil is very good at reflecting heat. It is used to make emergency sleeping bags and insulating wraps for newborn babies and marathon runners. Boilers are often insulated with aluminum foil.

Light and strong

Window frames, doors, and handrails can be made from aluminum, and it is used to make the wall cladding in large buildings. Aluminum is easier to handle than steel because of its low density. There is no need to paint it because aluminum does not rust. Aluminum alloys containing a little scandium or beryllium for added strength are used for the frames of backpacks, bicycles, and baseball bats. Aluminum ladders are lighter than traditional wooden ones, but they should not be used near overhead electricity cables because aluminum is a good conductor of electricity.

A good conductor of electricity

Copper conducts electricity better than aluminum, but aluminum is used for overhead electricity cables because it is much lighter. It is also widely used for underground cables and cables in tall buildings. Television antennas, satellite dishes, and the bases of electric light bulbs are made from aluminum as well.

◀ Baseball bats, ladders, and backpack and bicycle frames are often made from aluminum alloys because they are light and strong.

Traveling with Aluminum

Aluminium is used in the manufacture of many types of vehicle because its low **density** lessens their weight, reduces the amount of fuel they need, and helps to make them more manoeuvrable.

Aluminum alloys are also used in naval vessels and fast ferries like this one. The aluminum reduces the weight of the ship and it does not rust.

On the road

Steel is often used in road vehicles such as cars, trucks, and buses. However, vehicle engine and body parts made from aluminium resist rust and reduce the vehicle's weight. This enables trucks to carry heavier loads while staying under the legal weight limits that are in place to protect roads and bridges.

Go by train

Aluminium **alloys** are used extensively in railway carriages, underground trains and goods wagons. Less fuel is needed to move the trains because they are lighter. They also have better acceleration, which cuts down journey times. Carriages and wagons built from aluminium alloys last much longer than those built from steel because aluminium does not rust.

The *1903 Flyer*

Wilbur and Orville Wright's first airplane was built around a wooden frame, and its engine contained aluminum components to keep the weight down. It flew 260 meters (853 feet) near Kitty Hawk, North Carolina, on December 14, 1903.

Into the air and beyond

Aluminum alloys are widely used in aircraft to make them as light as possible so they can get off the ground! The large external fuel tank on the space shuttle is made from a strong but lightweight alloy of aluminum containing 4 percent copper and 1 percent lithium. A similar alloy called duralumin is widely used in aircraft, cars, and other machinery. Invented by Alfred Wilm early in the 1900s, duralumin consists of aluminum containing about 4 percent copper, 1 percent magnesium, and a little manganese. It is easily worked into shape and becomes harder and stronger when heat-treated. Because aluminum alloys resist corrosion, airlines sometimes do not paint their aircraft, which reduces the weight even further.

Airships

The largest airship ever built was the *Hindenburg*. It was 245 meters (800 feet) long, had an aluminum frame, and was kept in the air by 200,000 cubic meters (7 million cubic feet) of flammable hydrogen. In 1937 the *Hindenburg* exploded at Lakehurst, New Jersey. The hydrogen was blamed for the explosion. However, the frame was covered by fabric containing aluminum powder and iron oxide, the same mixture used to weld railway lines together.

This is the famous airship, Hindenburg, which took four year to build and first flew in 1936. Its fabric skin contained aluminum powder and it had an aluminum alloy frame.

Aluminum Compounds

Alumina, or aluminum oxide, is the white powder from which aluminum is extracted. Another form of aluminum oxide is corundum, which forms attractive gemstones, including rubies and sapphires. Rubies are red because they contain small amounts of chromium, while sapphires are blue because they have small amounts of titanium and iron. Artificial rubies and sapphires have been made since the early 1900s, not just because they make attractive jewelry, but because they are very hard. The moving parts in mechanical watches often contain rubies to stop them being worn away.

The red circles you can see here are ruby jewels in the bearings of an expensive mechanical watch. Rubies consist of aluminum oxide and provide smooth, hard-wearing surfaces that reduce the friction between the moving parts in the watch.

The first laser

An American scientist named Theodore Maiman built the first laser in 1960. It used a ruby rod and, not surprisingly, produced a beam of red laser light.

Aluminum oxide

The form of aluminum oxide called corundum is one of the hardest natural substances. It is widely used in sandblasting, which is a method for cleaning buildings or to prepare the surface of steelwork for painting. It is also used as the abrasive in cutting and grinding tools for use on materials such as concrete.

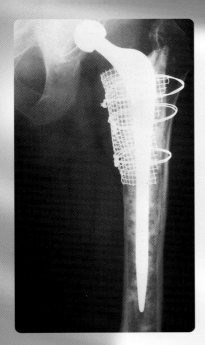

Aluminum oxide can be pressed into shape and heated to produce tough components that resist wear. The spark plugs in car engines contain aluminum oxide, and artificial hip joints may be lined with it.

◀ *This X-ray photograph shows an artificial hip joint in place at the top of a leg. The hip is a ball-and-socket joint and the socket may be lined with aluminum oxide to provide a smooth, but tough, surface.*

Aluminum chloride

Aluminum chloride is a white solid used as a catalyst by industry for manufacturing chemicals such as polystyrene, a plastic used to make cases for television sets and other electrical devices. Expanded polystyrene, containing bubbles of air, is used to make insulating carry-out containers. Hydrated aluminum chloride (also called aluminum chlorohydrate) is used in antiperspirants. Once it has been applied to the skin, it forms aluminum oxide, which plugs the pores in the skin, stopping the sweat from getting out. Dry aluminum chloride is not used because it reacts with water to produce a lot of heat and hydrochloric acid!

Aluminum hydroxide

Your stomach produces hydrochloric acid to provide the acidic conditions needed to digest proteins. It also kills harmful bacteria that might be in your food. However, if your stomach produces too much acid, you can get indigestion. Medicines called antacids help to cure indigestion by reacting with the extra acid. Aluminum hydroxide is often used as an antacid. When you swallow some, it reacts with the hydrochloric acid, helping you feel better.

The equation for the reaction of aluminum hydroxide with hydrochloric acid is

aluminum hydroxide + hydrochloric acid → aluminum chloride + water

$$Al(OH)_3(aq) + 3HCl(aq) \rightarrow AlCl_3(s) + 3H_2O(l)$$

Aluminum and Living Things

Water from rivers and reservoirs contains algae and tiny bits of various minerals, that make the water cloudy and taste bad. Before people can drink the water, these substances must be removed. Aluminum sulfate is used in water-treatment plants as a flocculating agent, which means it sticks these bits together. The clumps of unwanted material settle to the bottom and are removed along with the aluminum sulfate. This is important because soluble aluminum compounds are poisonous to plants and animals.

The Camelford incident

In 1988, 20 tons of aluminum sulfate was accidentally spilled into the wrong tank at a water-treatment plant, contaminating the water supply of the small English town of Camelford. The water tasted awful and was acidic because of the aluminum sulfate. The acid dissolved compounds of copper and other metals from the water pipes before they could be flushed clean, causing some people's hair and laundry to turn green or blue. Hundreds of people suffered skin rashes, arthritic pains, and memory loss.

Aluminum and acid rain

Coal and oil contain sulfur compounds that produce sulfur dioxide gas when they are burned. If this gas escapes into the atmosphere, it dissolves in the clouds to produce acid rain. Rain is naturally acidic because it contains some dissolved carbon dioxide, but the sulfur dioxide can make it as acidic as lemon juice! The acid damages the waxy layer on leaves of trees and other plants, and it dissolves aluminum compounds in the soil when it falls on the ground. Once the aluminum is dissolved, it is absorbed by plants through their roots, poisoning them. If aluminum gets washed into rivers and lakes, it can poison the animals and plants that live in them. If we are exposed to extra aluminum, our kidneys usually remove it from our bodies.

This girl is receiving kidney dialysis treatment because her kidneys have failed. Modern dialysis is very safe, but in the past dissolved aluminum compounds were sometimes present in the dialysis fluid, which caused some patients to suffer from temporary memory loss.

Acid rain has damaged these trees in a forest in North Carolina. The acid rain dissolves aluminum compounds in the soil, which poisons the trees and other plants.

Aluminum and dementia

Aluminum can build up in the bodies of people who suffer from kidney failure because their kidneys cannot filter waste substances from the blood. In the early days of dialysis, a process used to remove unwanted substances from blood, some people suffered from memory loss called dialysis dementia. This happened because the water used in the machines sometimes contained dissolved aluminum. Fortunately, dialysis dementia is reversible, and modern dialysing fluids do not contain aluminum.

Some people develop Alzheimer's disease as they get older. Alzheimer's is a very upsetting disease because eventually sufferers are unable to recognize their family or care for themselves. It was thought that aluminum caused Alzheimer's disease because it caused dialysis dementia. However, the two illnesses are very different, and today few scientists believe that aluminum causes Alzheimer's.

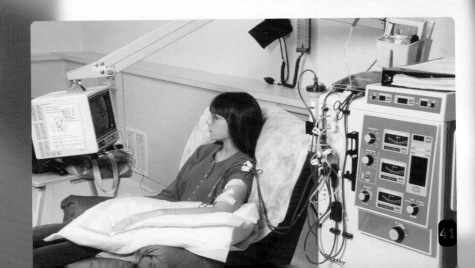

Gallium

Gallium is a silvery metal that is soft enough to cut with a knife. Gallium reacts slowly with acids, forming a layer of gallium oxide on its surface when it is exposed to air. This layer keeps the gallium underneath from reacting with air and water.

Melts in the hand

Gallium has a very low melting point compared to most metals. It melts at just 29.7 °C (85.5 °F), so you could melt it with the warmth from your hand. Most liquids contract when they are cooled and solidify. However, gallium expands, just as water does when it turns into ice.

▲

Gallium has a very low melting point compared with most metals. As you can see here, the warmth from a hand is enough to melt it.

Discovery of gallium

Paul-Emile Lecoq studied the spectrum of light emitted by some zinc ore when it was heated and found two previously unknown violet lines in 1875. This suggested that an unknown element was present. Lecoq isolated gallium metal later that year by passing electricity through a solution of gallium hydroxide ($Ga(OH)_3$).

Eka-aluminum

When Dimitri Mendeleev developed his periodic table in 1871, he left gaps for elements that he thought had not yet been discovered. He left one gap below aluminum for a missing element that he called eka-aluminum, which means "below aluminum." Mendeleev made predictions about the properties of eka-aluminum by looking at those of the surrounding elements in the periodic table. One of his predictions was that eka-aluminum would have a density of 5.9 g/cm^3. When gallium was discovered four years later, it was the missing eka-aluminum. Lecoq measured its density and found that it matched Mendeleev's predicted density almost exactly. This was a great success for Mendeleev's periodic table.

Gallium in the ground

On average, each ton of rock in the Earth's crust contains just 19 grams (0.7 ounce) of gallium within various compounds. Gallium is found in rare minerals such as gallite (copper gallium sulfide) and sohngeite (gallium hydroxide). However, most gallium is extracted from bauxite, which is aluminum ore. On average, each ton of bauxite contains about 50 grams (1.8 ounces) of gallium, which is taken out when the bauxite is purified for aluminum extraction. Only about 100 tons of gallium are produced in the world each year. This might not sound like a lot, but gallium is mainly used for making electronic devices, so only tiny amounts are needed.

This is a piece of bauxite. Most gallium is extracted from bauxite, which is actually an aluminum ore.

Uses of Gallium

In the past, mercury was used in most thermometers because it is liquid at room temperature and expands evenly when warmed up. Unfortunately, it is a poisonous metal, so other liquids, such as alcohol, are now often used instead. Gallium's low melting point can be lowered even further if it is mixed with other metals. One such alloy, containing gallium, indium, and tin, melts at −20 °C (−4 °F). It is used in a range of mercury-free thermometers for medical use, which are much safer than ordinary mercury thermometers. However, most gallium is used for making electronic devices.

Gallium arsenide

Gallium that contains tiny amounts of arsenic forms a semiconductor called gallium arsenide. This is a very important material because computer chips based on it are much faster than those made using silicon. The biggest single use for gallium is to make fast electronic devices, such as radar transmitters. In addition, gallium arsenide can be used to make solar cells, light-emitting diodes (LEDs), and other electronic components because it is light sensitive. This means that light is converted into electricity when it falls on gallium arsenide. Conversely, if electricity is passed through gallium arsenide, light is given off.

Gallium arsenide ▶ in used in fast computer chips for electronic devices such as radar.

Semiconductors and doping

Semiconductors are poor conductors of electricity at room temperature. But they become better conductors at higher temperatures or when tiny amounts of other elements are added to them. This is called doping. Silicon, doped with elements such as gallium or arsenic, is the best known semiconductor. It is widely used to make silicon chips for computers and other electronic devices.

Lovely light

Solar cells are devices that convert light (usually sunlight) directly into electricity. Many of them contain gallium arsenide. Small solar cells are often used to power pocket calculators and many devices in remote areas, such as public telephone booths and road signs. Solar cells can provide electricity only while the Sun is shining on them, so rechargeable batteries are needed to keep the electricity flowing at night. In space, large panels made from many solar cells power satellites and space probes.

Small electronic components called light-emitting diodes (LEDs) contain materials such as gallium arsenide and gallium nitride. LEDs give off light when electricity is passed through them and are more efficient than ordinary light bulbs because they release far less energy as heat. They are used in giant outdoor display screens, bicycle lights, and digital displays for electrical equipment such as video recorders. Lasers based on gallium arsenide are used in CD and DVD players to read the digital information on the disks.

▲

Gallium arsenide is used in many solar cells. In remote areas, solar cells provide the electricity to power road signs and telephone booths, such as this one in Nevada.

Indium

Indium is a silvery metal. It is softer than lead and is easily worked into shape, even at very low temperatures. Indium does not react with oxygen in the air unless it is heated strongly, and then it burns to form yellow indium oxide (In_2O_3). Although it reacts with acids, indium does not react with water.

▲
These are pieces of soft, silvery indium metal.

Discovery of indium

Indium was discovered in 1863 by Ferdinand Reich and Theodor Richter. During some chemical experiments on a sample of zinc ore, they made an unusual yellow solid, which led them to believe that the ore contained a new element. To confirm their discovery, Richter used a spectrometer to study the spectrum of light given off when the yellow solid was heated. The spectrum contained an indigo line.

Rare indium

There is very little indium in the Earth's crust. On average there may be less than 1 gram (0.04 ounce) of indium in every 10 tons of rock, so it is about as rare as silver. Indium is contained in rare minerals such as indite (iron indium sulfide), roquesite (copper indium sulfide) and dzhalindite (indium hydroxide). Over a third of the world's reserves of minerals that contain indium are found in Canada. Although China has smaller reserves of indium, it is the biggest producer of indium in the world. About 300 tons of indium are produced in the world each year, and a third of it comes from China. Indium is usually extracted from the waste material left over from processing zinc ore, especially sphalerite (zinc sulfide). The process is complex and involves several stages that take up to two months to complete. These include electrolysis and extraction with various chemicals. The indium extracted is mostly 99.97 percent pure, but for electronic uses it may be further purified to 99.999 percent or better.

Mirror, mirror ...

When indium melts, the molten metal clings easily to other substances, such as glass and metals. Mirrors are made by coating glass with molten aluminum or silver. When the metal solidifies, it forms a shiny surface that reflects most of the light that falls on it, hardly changing the color or shape at all. Mirrors made by coating glass with indium do not corrode easily, as silver does and are even better at reflecting light than either aluminum or silver.

This is sphalerite (zinc sulfide), which is the main source of indium.

Uses of Indium

Indium has some very unusual and useful properties. It is a metal that stays soft even at extremely low temperatures and it can stick to itself without needing to be heated first, a process called cold welding. A third of the indium produced is mixed with other metals to produce a wide range of alloys that also have many uses.

Brush regularly

If you have too many sweets and carbonated drinks, you may suffer from tooth decay. Although regular brushing helps, bacteria and the acids they produce may damage the hard outer layer of the tooth. Dentists remove the decayed part of the tooth and fill the hole left behind. Many modern tooth fillings are made from a white plastic material called resin. However, fillings made from a mixture of mercury, silver, and other metals are still very common because they are long lasting and cheap. It is very important that the metal filling does not shrink as it hardens because any gaps left would let bacteria and acids back in, causing decay all over again. Small amounts of indium are used in the mixture to produce a hard alloy that shrinks very little.

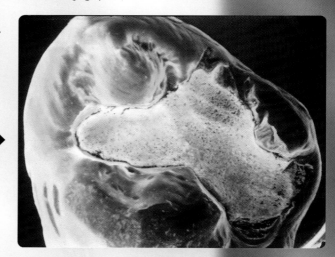

This is a tooth with a filling made from a mixture of mercury and silver, seen through an electron microscope. Metal dental fillings may also contain small amounts of indium to improve the properties of the filling.

Sticking and sealing

Many indium alloys melt at low temperatures, making them useful as solders for joining electronic components. Electronic components are attached to printed circuit boards with an alloy that contains 52 percent indium and 48 percent tin and melts at just 118 °C (244 °F). This does not damage the components or the board because it melts at a low temperature.

Indium also resists corrosion. That is why indium alloys are used in electrical fuses. If an electric device becomes faulty, too much current could flow, which is dangerous. The high current causes the metal in the fuse to heat up and melt. This breaks the circuit and blocks the flow of electricity.

Indium alloys are used as solders for joining electronic components together on printed circuit boards. They melt at low temperatures and do not corrode easily.

A strange alloy

Indium melts at 156 °C (313 °F), and gallium melts at 29.7 °C (85.5 °F). However, a mixture of 24.5 percent indium and 75.5 percent gallium melts at just 16.5 °C (61.7 °F)! Such indium alloys are useful for holding glass or plastic lenses while they are being ground to the correct shape because they can be released easily by gently warming the alloy.

It is often very difficult to get a tight seal between two different materials, such as metal and glass. When they are heated and cooled they expand and contract by different amounts, causing gaps to appear between them. However, indium sticks to metal and glass and forms a tight seal whether it is heated, cooled, or shaken by vibrations. Indium seals are widely used in vacuum pumps and equipment that must work at low temperatures.

Indium Compounds

Indium phosphide is a semiconductor material consisting of indium and tiny amounts of phosphorus. Like gallium arsenide, it is used in high-speed electronic circuits and solar cells. Only small amounts of indium are used in this way.

Indium-tin oxide

Special coatings that contain indium oxide account for about half of the indium produced. Very thin layers of indium oxide are transparent and can conduct electricity. Indium-tin oxide (ITO) contains about 90 percent indium oxide and 10 percent tin oxide. ITO conducts electricity better than indium oxide on its own and thin layers of it are also transparent. These properties make ITO a very useful material in many ways.

No more frosty windows

In winter, windows of vehicles can become coated on the outside with thick frost. When we get inside, things often get even worse, water vapor in our breath condenses on the glass, misting up the windows and making it impossible to see out. ITO-coated glass is easily de-iced and de-misted within a short time, just by passing electricity from the car battery through the ITO layer. The ITO layer does not interfere with visibility because it is transparent. This glass is widely used in train and aircraft windshields and for making frost-free glass doors for commercial food freezers.

The windshields of trains, airplanes, and helicopters may be coated with a very thin, transparent layer of indium-tin oxide. When electricity is passed through the layer, it warms up and removes any frost or mist from the glass, providing a clear view in cold weather.

Keep your cool

Buildings with many windows can become unbearably hot in the summer because infrared light from the Sun passes through the glass into the rooms. We cannot see infrared light, but we do feel it as heat. Thin layers of indium-tin oxide let visible light through, but stop infrared light. Buildings that have ITO-coated glass in the windows warm up less in the summer because the infrared light that passes through the windows is reduced. It is more comfortable inside and there is less need to use air-conditioning equipment. As a result, energy is not wasted keeping the building cool.

Liquid crystal displays

Liquid crystal displays (LCDs) are used in all kinds of electrical devices. These include the flat screens used in laptop computers, CD players, electronic handheld games, digital watches, and calculators. When light passes through liquid crystals, it is twisted. However when electricity flows through liquid crystals, they change shape and cannot twist the light as much, producing a dark area in the display. One of the layers in the display is ITO-coated glass, which conducts electricity to the liquid crystals. Some computer displays are touch-sensitive and can detect your finger when you touch the screen. These have a thin coating of ITO on the outer surface.

Liquid crystal displays (LCDs) contain a layer of glass coated with indium-tin oxide. LCDs are widely used in calculators, digital watches, CD players, and other electronic devices.

Thallium

Thallium is a soft metal. It reacts with oxygen in the air to form a thick layer of blue-gray thallium oxide. However, if this layer is cut away, the surface is silvery with a blue tinge. Thallium does not react with water, but it does react with steam to form thallium hydroxide and hydrogen gas. Thallium reacts slowly with sulfuric acid and hydrochloric acid.

Not three, just one

When elements in group 13 react with other elements such as chlorine, the compounds formed have similar chemical formulas. Boron chloride is BCl_3 and aluminum chloride is $AlCl_3$, for example. However, thallium compounds are different. Thallium chloride, for instance, is TlCl, with just one chlorine atom for each thallium atom instead of three.

Discovery of thallium

The English scientist Sir William Crookes discovered thallium in 1861. Crookes was actually interested in selenium compounds and was heating some waste left over from sulfuric acid production, which is where selenium is normally found. When he examined the spectrum of light produced, he found an unexpected green line. It wasn't selenium that Crookes had found, but a new element, which he named thallium after the Greek word meaning "green twig." Crookes and a French chemist named Claude-Auguste Lamy both managed to isolate thallium in 1862, and each showed that it was a metal.

This is the English scientist Sir William Crookes (1832–1919), who discovered thallium in 1861 and invented the radiometer. He is seen here holding another one of his inventions, the Crookes tube, which he used to investigate cathode rays. ▶

The Crookes radiometer

William Crookes measured the atomic mass of thallium using a vacuum balance. However, when light shined on it, he got slightly different readings. He investigated this further and as a result he invented his radiometer. This is a glass bulb containing very little air and a rotor with four metal vanes. One side of each vane is black and the other side is shiny. When sunlight shines on the vanes, the black sides warm up more than the shiny sides. The air molecules next to the black sides absorb some of the heat and bounce off the vanes, causing the rotor to spin very quickly. The Crookes radiometer has little practical use but is an interesting toy.

Thallium production

Thallium compounds are found in several rare minerals such as crooksite, lorandite, and hutchinsonite, but the pure metal is not found naturally. Thallium is rare in the Earth's crust, and on average each ton of rock contains only about 0.5 gram (0.02 ounce) of thallium compounds. Only about 15 tons of thallium and its compounds are extracted in the world each year. Rather than trying to extract thallium from its minerals, it is obtained from waste material left over after zinc production, just as indium is. Several steps are needed, and thallium metal is eventually produced by passing electricity through a solution of thallium compounds.

Uses of Thallium

Thallium metal itself has no real commercial use. An alloy of mercury and thallium is used in thermometers for measuring low temperatures because it freezes at −59 °C (−74.2 °F), 20 Celsius degrees (11 Fahrenheit degrees) lower than mercury alone. Most thallium is used in various thallium compounds.

Bending light

When a ray of light passes from one transparent substance into another, such as from air into glass, it changes direction slightly. This is called refraction. The larger the refractive index of the transparent substance, the more the light bends. Lenses are shaped in such a way that the light is focused. They are important parts of many things, including eyeglasses, microscopes, and telescopes. Glass containing thallium oxide has a larger refractive index than ordinary glass, so it bends light more, allowing thinner lenses to be made.

The thalofide cell

Thallium sulfide (Tl_2S) forms blue-black crystals, which are used in some photocells. Photocells are electronic devices that are sensitive to light. When light shines on the photocell, a small electric current flows, which stops when the light source is removed. The thalofide cell was invented in 1917 by two Americans, Theodore Case and Earl Sponable, and is sensitive to infrared light. Thalofide cells contain thallium oxy-sulfide, which is thallium sulfide with some sulfur atoms replaced by oxygen atoms. They were used by the United States Navy during World War I as part of a secret signaling system based on invisible infrared light. Simple Morse code was used at first, but the system was later developed to carry voice signals between ships nearly 20 kilometers (12.5 miles) apart.

Infrared spectroscopy

Infrared spectroscopy is a method used by chemists to analyze chemicals. Various chemicals absorb infrared light in different ways, and every chemical has its own fingerprint. Crystals containing thallium bromide and thallium iodide are very good at letting infrared light pass through. They are used to make lenses and other parts of infrared spectrometers.

Not just movies—talkies too!

Case and Sponable's thalofide cell was the basis of Movietone, one of the first methods for adding sound to movies. The soundtrack was recorded as a series of dark lines on one side of the film. When the film was shown, a thalofide cell converted the pattern of lines into a series of electrical pulses, which were used to power a loudspeaker. The first Movietone News stories, complete with sound, were shown in 1927.

Gamma ray detectors

Gamma rays are similar to X rays, but more powerful. They are found in cosmic rays from space, so astronomers are very interested in studying them. Sodium iodide crystals containing small amounts of thallium emit a flash of light whenever gamma rays pass through them. They are used in gamma ray detectors in space probes and gamma ray telescopes.

▼ *Gamma rays can be detected using sodium iodide crystals containing small amounts of thallium. Such crystals were used in this space telescope, called the Compton Gamma Ray Observatory, which was launched into orbit from the space shuttle in 1991.*

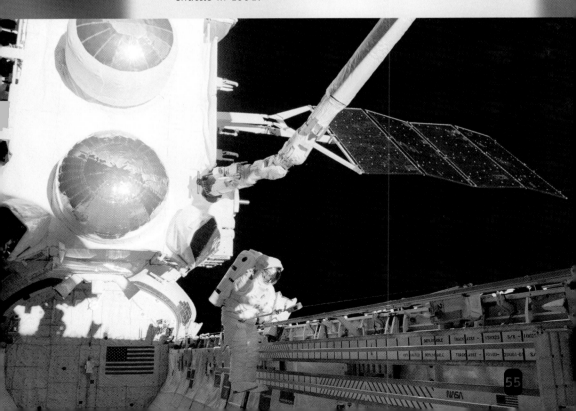

Thallium and Health

Thallium is a dense metal and one of its compounds, thallium acetate, is used to make liquids with a high density. These liquids are used by the metal refining industry to separate the different minerals in ores. Crushed rock is mixed with the dense liquid, and many bubbles are blown through. This produces froth at the surface that contains some minerals, while others sink to the bottom. However, soluble thallium compounds like this must be handled carefully because they are poisonous.

Ringworm and rats

Ringworm is a fungal skin infection that causes itchy red rashes that look like rings. It is quite contagious and is spread by contact with infected pets, people, combs, and clothing. Modern antifungal creams help to treat ringworm safely, but in the past thallium acetate and thallium sulfate were used. Although they were effective, they were also poisonous and were often used as rat poison, too!

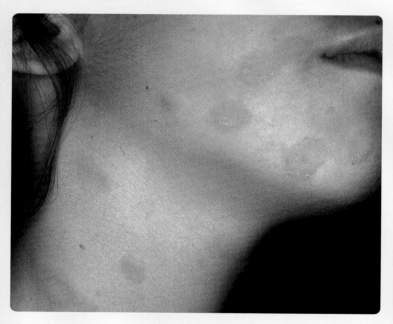

▲
The red rings on this person's skin are caused by a fungal infection called ringworm. Thallium compounds were used to cure ringworm in the past, but they are no longer used because they are too poisonous.

Poisonous thallium

Many countries have banned the use of thallium compounds if safer alternatives exist. In 1972 the United States banned the use of thallium compounds in rat poison, and they are no longer used to treat ringworm. If someone swallows a large dose of thallium compound, they suffer from vomiting, diarrhea, and possibly hair loss after about two weeks. In severe cases they may die. However, thallium is still used in modern medicine.

Thallium in cardiac scans

Thallium-201 is an artificial isotope. It is radioactive and gives off radiation, such as X rays. Doctors use thallium-210 to study the blood flow of patients with heart disease. When a patient has a cardiac scan with thallium-201, a tiny amount is injected into a vein. The thallium-201 goes wherever the blood flows and the radiation it emits is easily detected by a handheld scanner. The doctor may compare a scan of the heart after the patient has exercised on a treadmill with one taken while the patient is resting. This helps the doctor find out if there are any areas in the heart not getting enough blood.

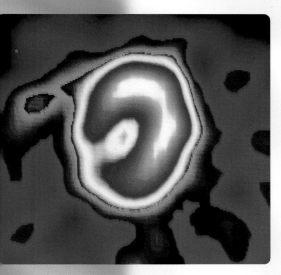

◀ This is a thallium scan of a normal human heart. The pink and red areas show where the thallium has concentrated in the heart muscle. Scans like this help doctors diagnose problems that may lead to heart attacks.

Isotopes

Isotopes are atoms of an element that have the same number of protons and electrons, but different numbers of neutrons. Most elements found naturally have a small number of different isotopes mixed together, but scientists are able to make artificial isotopes in nuclear reactors and machines called particle accelerators.

57

Find Out More About the Group 13 Elemen

The table below contains information about the properties of the elements of group 13 .

Element	Symbol	Atomic number	Melting point (°C)	Boiling point (°C)	State at 25 °C	State at 30 °C	Density at 25°C (g/cm³)
boron	B	5	2076	3927	solid	solid	2.3
aluminum	Al	13	660	2520	solid	solid	2.7
gallium	Ga	31	29.7	2403	solid	liquid	5.9
indium	In	49	156	2072	solid	solid	7.3
thallium	Tl	81	304	1473	solid	solid	11.8

Compounds

These tables show you the chemical formulas of most of the compounds mentioned in this book. For example, boron oxide has the formula B_2O_3. This means it is made from two boron atoms and three oxygen atoms joined together by chemical bonds.

Boron compounds

Boron compound	formula
borax	$Na_2B_4O_7 \cdot 10H_2O$
colemanite	$CaB_3O_4(OH)_3 \cdot H_2O$
kernite	$Na_2B_4O_6(OH)_2 \cdot 3H_2O$
boric acid	H_3BO_3
boron carbide	B_4C
boron chloride	BCl_3
boron nitride	BN
boron oxide	B_2O_3
diborane	B_2H_6
sodium borate	Na_3BO_3

Aluminum compound	formula
bauxite	Al_2O_3
cryolite	Na_3AlF_6
aluminum chloride	$AlCl_3$
aluminum chlorohydrate	$AlCl_3 \cdot 6H_2O$
aluminum hydroxide	$Al(OH)_3$
aluminum oxide	Al_2O_3
aluminum sulfate	$Al_2(SO_4)_3$
potassium aluminum sulfate	$KAl(SO_4)_2 \cdot 12H_2O$

Aluminum compounds

Gallium compound	formula
gallite	$CuGaS_2$
sohngeite	$Ga(OH)_3$
gallium arsenide	$GaAs$
gallium nitride	GaN

Gallium compounds

Indium compound	formula
dzhalindite	$In(OH)_3$
indite	$Fe^{2+}In_2S_4$
roquesite	$CuInS_2$
indium oxide	In_2O_3
indium phosphide	InP

Indium compounds

Thallium compound	formula
thallium (I) chloride	$TlCl$
crookesite	$Cu_7(Tl,Ag)Se_4$
lorandite	$TlAsS_2$
hutchinsonite	$(Pb,Tl)_2As_5S_9$
thallium (I) acetate	CH_3COOTl
thallium (I) iodide	TlI
thallium (I) bromide	$TlBr$
thallium (I) hydroxide	$TlOH$
thallium (I) oxide	Tl_2O
thallium (I) sulfide	Tl_2S
thallium (I) sulfate	Tl_2SO_4

Thallium compounds

Acids

Acid	formula
boric acid	H_3BO_3
hydrochloric acid	HCl
nitric acid	HNO_3
sulfuric acid	H_2SO_4

Other compounds

Compounds	formula
ammonia	NH_3
ammonium perchlorate	NH_4ClO_4
iron (II) oxide	Fe_2O_3
sodium iodide	NaI
tin (II) oxide	SnO
water	H_2O
zinc sulfide	ZnS

◄ This is sphalerite (zinc sulfide), which is the main practical source of indium.

Glossary

alloy mixture of two or more metals, or a mixture of a metal and a nonmetal

atom smallest particle of an element that has the properties of that element

atomic number number of protons in the nucleus of an atom

bond force that joins atoms together

compound substance made from the atoms of two or more elements, joined together by chemical bonds

density mass of a substance compared to its volume (how much space it takes up). To find the density or a substance, you divide its mass by its volume. Substances with a high density feel very heavy for their size.

DNA (deoxyribonucleic acid) long, complex chemical that carries the genetic information and is the substance of inheritance for almost all living things

electrolysis breaking down or decomposing a compound by passing electricity through it. The compound must be molten or dissolved in a liquid for electrolysis to work.

electron particle in an atom that has a negative electric charge. Electrons are found in shells around the nucleus of an atom.

element substance made from only one type of atom

extract to remove a chemical from a mixture of chemicals

fertilizer chemical that gives plants the elements they need for healthy growth

group vertical column of elements in the periodic table. Elements in a group have similar properties.

herbicide chemical that kills unwanted plants, usually weeds

isotope atoms of an element with the same number of protons and electrons, but a different number of neutrons

mineral substance that is found naturally in the earth but does not come from animals or plants. Metal ores and limestone are examples of minerals.

neutron particle in an atom's nucleus that does not have an electric charge

nuclear reaction reaction involving the nucleus of an atom. Radiation is produced in nuclear reactions.

nucleus central part of an atom made from protons and neutrons. It has a positive electric charge.

ore substance containing minerals from which metals can be taken out and purified

period horizontal row of elements in the periodic table

periodic table chart in which all the known elements are arranged into groups and periods

pesticide chemical that kills insects

prism block of transparent material, usually glass, that has a triangular cross-section

proton particle in a atom's nucleus that has a positive electric charge

radioactive producing radiation

radiation energy or particles given off when an atom decays

reaction chemical change that produces new substances

refining removing impurities from a substance to make it more pure. It can also mean separating the different substances in a mixture, for example, in oil refining.

semiconductor substance, such as silicon, that is an electrical insulator at room temperature, but a conductor when it is warmed or other elements are added to it

soluble substance that will dissolve

spectrometer piece of equipment that splits the light given off by something into its spectrum

spectrum different colors that make up a ray of light. Different colors of light have different spectra.

subatomic particle particle smaller than an atom, such as a proton, neutron, or electron

vacuum empty space containing very little air or none at all

welding joining two or more metals together, usually by heating them

Timeline

boron discovered	1808	Sir Humphry Davy, Joseph-Louis Gay-Lussac, and Louis-Jaques Thénard
aluminum discovered	1825	Hans Christian Oersted
thallium discovered	1861	Sir William Crookes
indium discovered	1863	Ferdinand Reich and Theodor Richter
gallium discovered	1875	Paul-Emile Lecoq
industrial extraction of aluminum invented	1886	Charles Hall and Paul Héroult
first laser built	1960	Theodore Maiman

Further Reading and Useful Websites

Books

Oxlade, Chris. *Elements and Compounds*. Chicago: Heinemann Library, 2002.

Oxlade, Chris. *Metals*. Chicago: Heinemann Library, 2002.

Websites

WebElements™
http://www.webelements.com
An interactive periodic table crammed with information and photographs.

DiscoverySchool
http://school.discovery.com/clipart
Help for science projects and homework and free science clip art.

Proton Don
http://www.funbrain.com/periodic
The fun periodic table quiz!

BBC Science
http://www.bbc.co.uk/science
Quizzes, news, information and games about all areas of science.

Creative Chemistry
http://www.creative chemistry.org.uk
An interactive chemistry site with fun practical activities, quizzes, puzzles and more.

Index